Quilting with Carol Armstrong

30 Quilting Patterns ❋ Appliqué Designs ❋ 16 Projects

Carol Armstrong

C&T PUBLISHING

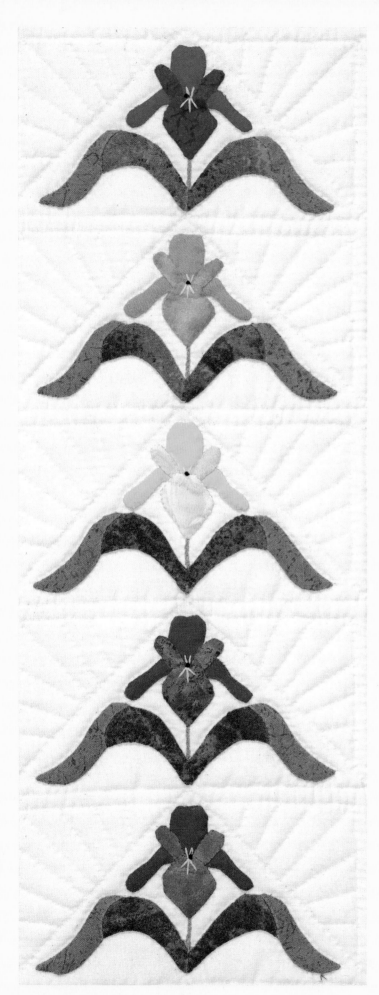

© 2001 Carol Armstrong

Front Cover: Detail of *Grandmother's Fan*, Carol Armstrong

Back Cover: Churn Dash, Carol Armstrong

Developmental Editor: Barbara Konzak Kuhn

Technical Editor: Karyn Hoyt

Copy Editor, Proofreader: Lucy Grijalva, Carol Barrett

Cover Designer: Aliza Kahn Shalit

Book Designer: Rose Sheifer

Design Director: Diane Pedersen

Illustrator: Kirstie L. McCormick

Production Assistant: Tim Manibusan

Photography: Steve Buckley Photograhic Reflections; photos on pages 6, 12-21 by Sharon Risedorph

Library of Congress Cataloging-in-Publication Data

Armstrong, Carol,
  Quilting with Carol Armstrong : 30 quilting patterns, applique designs, 16 projects / Carol Armstrong.
     p. cm.
Includes bibliographical references and index.
  ISBN 1-57120-170-X (paper trade)
  1. Quilting--Patterns. 2. Appliqué--Patterns. I. Title.
  TT835 .A753 2001
  74646'041--dc21

                       2001002433

Published by C&T Publishing, Inc.
P. O. Box 1456
Lafayette, California 94549

Printed in China
10 9 8 7 6 5 4 3 2 1

Dedicated to
my Aunt Helen

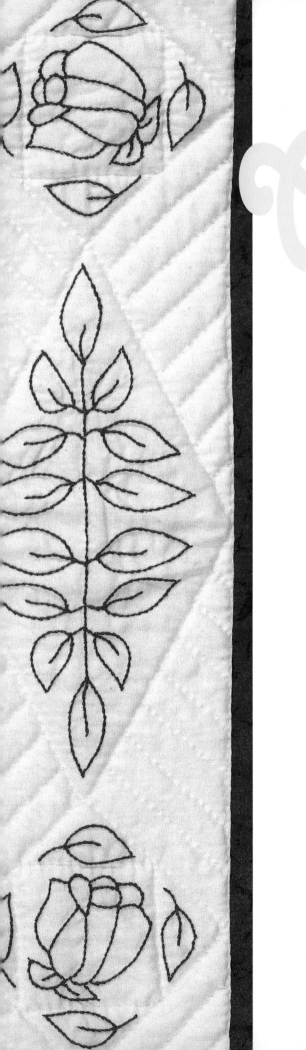

Contents

Projects

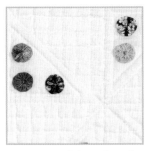

Yo-Yo Pinwheel,
page 24

Lacy Log Cabin,
page 28

Shoo-Fly,
page 32

Grandmother's
Little Angels,
page 36

Lonestar,
page 42

Attic Windows,
page 46

Cross Variation,
page 50

Storm at Sea,
page 54

Bow Ties,
page 58

Grandmother's Fan,
page 64

Churn Dash,
page 68

Maple Leaves,
page 72

Single Appliqué
Blocks,
Pages 78-91

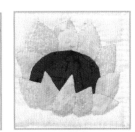

Introduction

Have you ever thought of quilting your block pattern instead of piecing it? Now, with this easy-to-learn technique, familiar patterns such as Bow Tie, Storm at Sea, or Grandmother's Fan take on a new look. There are no restrictions in the design possibilities. Any drawn line can be a quilting line. With the quilting creating the "block" design lines, there is plenty of room to play with your favorite stitchery to add color to the piece. Any unquilted area can be the "artist's canvas." Any idea is worth a few test sketches.

You can go beyond basic blocks and standard layouts by creating whole-cloth designs. Combinations of squares and triangles with borders can also become wonderful quilts. Get out that graph paper and give some a try.

I really enjoy this quilting style. The hand and feel of the richly quilted fabrics are wonderful. This style allows me to try many different surface techniques and to use the results in a complete project. And I have only just begun!

Happy Quilting!

Carol Armstrong

Getting Started

With my newest approach to creating quilts, you use quilting lines—rather than piecing—to define the block pattern. Then you enhance the design with embellishments or decorations of your choice, such as appliqué, embroidery, or painting.

This book offers twelve wonderful quilts and six more individual blocks that showcase block patterns to quilt and embellish using what I call the "Quilt First" and "Quilt Second" methods. The opening chapters will tell you everything you need to know—not only about how to make the projects in the book, but how to turn your favorite block pattern into a new version that will delight the eye.

DESIGN HINTS

If you want to create your own design or modify one of mine, here are some ideas: You can make a small quilt using a single block or you can repeat blocks any number of times to make a larger quilt. You can join blocks together with sashing, or you can butt the blocks together and create secondary designs where the edges meet. Experiment with paper drawings—pick a block design, then draw only the main quilt lines. Make copies of your block—enlarge or reduce the size if you wish, then arrange them until you have a design you like. Some quilt designs are simple such as a Four-Patch. Others, such as Mariner's Compass, are more complicated, but how wonderful it would be in a quilted version. It's on my list to try. *Making the Patterns* (pages 12 - 13) will guide you through this planning process.

Just as you would use different colors or printed fabrics to change the look of a pieced block, you can use different quilting designs and embellishments to change a quilted block. All the different versions are right: the biggest difficulty is deciding which to try first. Take a look at the *Color and Embellishment* techniques starting on page 14 for appliqué, painting, and stitching options.

Once you have a plan for decorating your block, you can choose between Quilt First and Quilt Second. If you use appliqué, embroidery, or paint, you will generally want to Quilt Second. Otherwise, you can Quilt First, then add embellishments such as beads, buttons, ribbons, or lace. The *Construction* section starting on page 16 covers both methods.

Whether you use one of my designs or create your own, you'll have a unique quilt to keep or give to a treasured friend. Try just one block or try them all, but have fun!

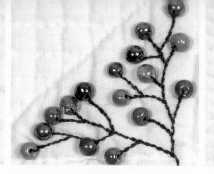

Materials and Supplies

DESIGN AND PATTERN MAKING

Graph Paper

I use 17" x 20" eight-squares-to-the-inch graph paper. The larger sheets work well for drafting whole projects. You can always tape several sheets together for grand projects.

Basic Drawing Tools

You should have: Pencils, a good eraser (for changing your mind), a straight edge, a ruler, permanent markers (when your mind is made up), and a compass for curves.

Lightbox

A lightbox is excellent for tracing repeated motifs when designing. I also use it to trace appliqué pieces as well as quilting and other designs. A window or a lamp under a glass table can be an adequate substitute if you don't have a lightbox.

Cutting Mat, Ruler, and Rotary Cutter

Cutting mats, rulers, and rotary cutters aren't just for cutting fabric. Because I feel it is most accurate, I use a rotary cutter and an older blade to cut the block templates I use to mark my designs on the background fabric. Accuracy in templates is important, because a small error in a block shape is amplified in a multi-block quilt. I also find that a cutting mat with grid lines is most useful.

Freezer Paper

Freezer paper can be used for marking patterns on the background fabric and for stabilizing fabric prior to painting it. Its ability to adhere to fabric with a touch of a medium-heat iron makes it ideal for accurate placement in some pattern transfers.

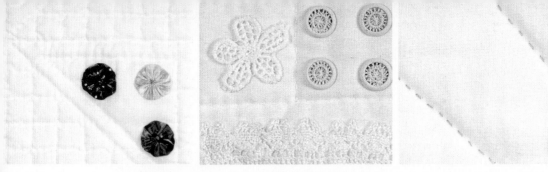

Template Plastic, Acetate Sheets, Card Stock

Template plastic, acetate sheets, and card stock work equally well for the block templates used for basic marking. They are all easy to cut with a rotary cutter.

Color Pencils, Crayons, Markers, Watercolors

Coloring your design sketch is a quick way to see the effect of different colors on the same design before you select your fabric.

SEWING

Fabrics

A good, utility muslin shows the quilting designs beautifully. I use a perma-press, pre-shrunk, 100% cotton, unbleached muslin. Light colors will also highlight the quilt designs. Or you can be daring and use a dark or black background and contrasting quilting thread. Use solids or near solids for the backgrounds, as patterns will detract from the quilting stitches. 100% cottons are best for quilting and appliqué, as they respond well to finger pressing and do what you ask of them. Color? We all know we need some of every fabric we see in the shops! Start your stash.

Thread

A cotton or cotton-wrapped polyester thread will fit most sewing needs. For quilting, however, you need a thread that is specifically designed for quilting. There are many brands and I have had success with most. Quilting with colored thread can add a new accent to your work. I predominantly use a natural color on the unbleached muslin. For basting, I use pure white. For registration marks, a pastel color is preferable.

Batting

For the best definition in your quilting, I find a needle-punch polyester works the best. (Specifically I use Poly-Fil® Traditional.) A cotton batting that is friendly to hand quilting creates nice patterns also. Try a small project with both types of batting and save them for reference.

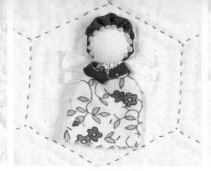

Spray Starch

Use one or two applications of spray starch on your background fabric before marking the appliqué or quilting. This slight stiffening keeps the background from distorting when sewing or marking. However, do not use it before any paint or dye technique, as it may interfere with adhesion.

Markers

I use a blue water-removable marker (very lightly) on the light colors. Light pencil is favored by some. *Do not iron any marks as they may set permanently.* Masking tape is my preferred marker for straight lines. To prevent any sticky residue, "de-sticky" it by placing it on some scrap fabric first, and then removing it before using it on your quilt. For short-term marking for quilting, press the tip of a needle into the fabric and "draw" it along—marking as you go.

Basic Sewing Supplies

Good scissors, needles, pins, and favorite thimbles fill out the basic needs. You will develop your own preference for tools as you sew. Do not be afraid to try something new.

Iron

A good steam iron is invaluable, of course.

SURFACE DESIGN

Quilting is the foundation, and many techniques can be used for color and embellishment. Basic appliqué, redwork, ribbon embroidery, and paper piecing can be enhanced with beads, buttons, and bows. Each requires its own supplies. Likewise, methods such as stenciling, stamping, photo transfer, painting, and dyeing require specific materials.

If you are like me, you have on your shelves, books that describe techniques you hope one day to incorporate into your quilts. Here is the perfect opportunity to try your hand at some new surface techniques or use an old favorite in a new way.

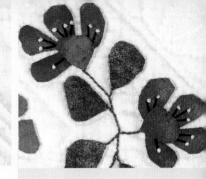

Important Project Tips

....
Tracing

You can darken the lines on your working pattern with a permanent marker to aid in tracing. Usually you can see through the muslin background, but if you have trouble, use a lightbox when marking the quilts.

....
Removable Marker

I use a blue water-removable marker for fabric. As with any marker, I use it lightly but visibly. To remove the marks after any process, I spray the work lightly with water in a spray bottle. Allow the fabric to dry thoroughly before pressing. Be sure to use scraps of your fabric and test removing your brand of marker before you use it on your project.

....
Pre-Washing

Because I use water to remove any marker, it is important to test for color-fastness with any fabric you use. I do not pre-wash any fabrics as a rule.

....
Working Patterns

Draw your working patterns on a letter-weight paper so that light from the lightbox can go through (especially when tracing appliqué fabric pieces).

Quilting Note: Quilting will cause your finished piece to be a bit smaller than the patterns.

....
Pressing

Use a bit of steam and a medium-heat iron for cotton fabrics. Do not pull or push the fabric, or it may warp. You will get a feel for it after a few projects.

....
Cutting Background Fabric

I have used one-inch extra all around when giving measurements in the projects. For your first few projects, you may want to give yourself two inches until you are more comfortable with the marking process.

Making the Patterns

You may wish to use one of the designs I have included or create one of your own from a favorite quilt block. In either case it is best to draw the design full size, using graph paper. The main lines of the block will be quilting lines–I have marked these in dashed lines. The solid lines mark where the applied designs will go.

First, draw the main block elements using a pencil and a ruler to draw straight lines. For an example, we will use the Pinwheel block.

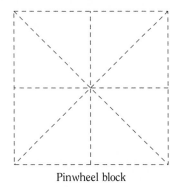

Pinwheel block

Second, decide which pieces of your block will contain applied designs and create these elements. In this case I designed a simple flower motif to fit the space.

Design to be applied

Note that you need only draw the full-size design once on a separate sheet of paper. Then using a lightbox, you will trace the design into each corresponding space. This is also true of the quilting patterns, which you will draw in the remaining spaces. It's best to avoid tiny design elements as they will get lost in the stitching. For the Pinwheel block example, I decided to use simple straight-line quilting.

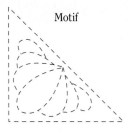
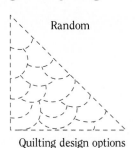
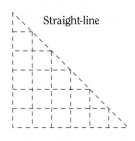

Motif   Random   Straight-line

Quilting design options

I will mention again that I use dashed lines for the quilting designs and solid lines for applied designs to avoid confusion when marking these elements for "what to quilt, what to color."

When I am happy with my pattern, I go over my pencil lines with a permanent marker. This now becomes my **working pattern**. I make a trip to the copier for several copies, and then begin coloring in my design. I usually try several color combinations. You may also want to use the copier to reduce your design—this will allow you to color your designs more quickly.

Working pattern

Before you begin sewing, you will need to cut a **block template** that is the size of your *finished* block. You will be using this block template to mark the **reference dots** for your quilted blocks on your background fabric. Make the template out of template plastic, acetate, or card stock. For accuracy, cut the template using a rotary cutter and a ruler on a gridded cutting mat. A few pieces of double-stick tape or rolled masking tape on the back of your chosen template material will keep it in place as you cut. After it is cut, mark the main quilting line reference dots on the template.

For our Pinwheel example, we will be able to mark the main quilting lines using the outside dots on the block template. This is true for most basic blocks. Any other needed lines will be traced from the working pattern. At a minimum, always mark the outer corners of a block so that you can realign the working pattern with your background fabric.

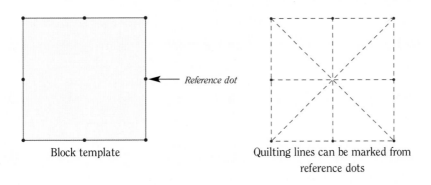

Block template

Quilting lines can be marked from reference dots

Color and Embellishment

BASIC APPLIQUÉ

Mark the appliqué design on the background fabric using a removable marker. A lightbox makes tracing this design from your working pattern easy. Then select the colors for each appliqué piece. Again using a lightbox, trace each individual appliqué piece onto the right side of the appliqué fabric with a removable marker. Cut out each piece leaving a 3/16" or so turn-under allowance.

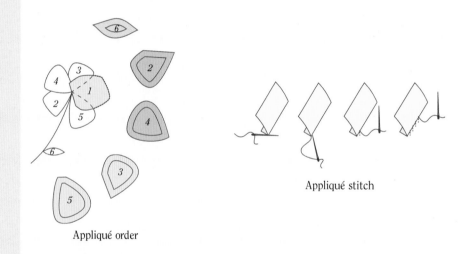

Appliqué order

Appliqué stitch

Before stitching, number the pattern for appliqué order. Pieces that are covered by another piece are sewn down first. Noting the order of appliqué on the pattern, stitch each piece onto the background using the pre-marked design as a guide. I use a tack stitch for appliqué.

Only turn under and sew those edges that are exposed, not those that will be covered by another piece. The lines on the background fabric guide the placement of each piece. As you stitch, use the needle to turn under the allowance to the line on the appliqué piece, matching it with the motif lines marked on the background fabric.

BASIC PAINTING

I use a fabric-ready acrylic paint, which is available at most hobby and craft stores. I begin my design by tracing the outline onto the background fabric with a permanent pigment pen, such as a Pigma®. Using a stiff brush, I apply my paints in a thin layer, allowing them to dry between colors (acrylics dry quickly). If my outline marks get painted over, I will redefine them afterward, along with any detail I may add, with a permanent marker or paint pen. Set the paint according to the directions on the paint container.

This is a wide-open technique with lots of fun possibilities. Try experimenting on some scrap fabrics. I find ironing fabric to the shiny side of freezer paper gives me a nice foundation. Use a medium-heat iron. The paper-foundation peels off the back easily after you are finished.

REDWORK EMBROIDERY

Whether red, blue, black, or green, single color outline embroidery can make quite a statement. I only use a few simple stitches–the outline or stem stitch, a French knot, and plain stitches.

French Knot

This creates great flower centers, with one or many in a cluster. It also creates tiny heads at the end of flowers stamens.

Bring the needle up from the wrong side of fabric. Wrap floss around the needle twice and insert the needle back into the fabric close to the thread's exit. Pull the knot tight (but not too tight) and pull the needle through, holding the knot until all the floss is pulled through.

Note: You can increase the size of the knot by using more strands of floss.

French knot

Stem Stitch

Just like it sounds, it makes thin stems, as well as any fine lines such as a stamen. To make the stems thicker, stitch two or more lines next to one another.

Stem stitch

Mark the design of your choice on the background fabric with pencil or a removable marker and embroider. You may wish to use a hoop to hold the fabric taut, or spray the background fabric with several applications of spray starch. I prefer the starch. After the embroidery is complete, remove any marker and press from the back.

Construction

There are two ways a quilted-block quilt is constructed. Number one, the simplest, is **Quilt First**, then add decoration such as lace, beads, or buttons. Number two is apply your decoration (appliqué, paint, embroidery) first, and **Quilt Second**. Your choice of applied design will determine which method is best. In most cases appliqué, paint, and embroidery are best done with Quilt Second, while beads, buttons, and lace work best with Quilt First. I have used both techniques as examples in this book.

QUILT FIRST

The Yo-Yo Pinwheel quilt is an example of Quilt First. Because you will not need to do any pressing until after the quilting is done, you can mark all the quilting lines with removable marker, do your quilting, then remove the marks before pressing. (For instructions on making the Yo-Yo Pinwheel quilt, see page 24.)

The first step is to determine how big your finished quilt will be and cut your background fabric at least 1" larger on all sides. Press, using a bit of spray starch to make it more stable (see page 10). Use a ruler or yardstick to draw a line along one side of the background fabric at least 1" from the edge. This is your **main line** and will give you the base line for marking your blocks. Place your block template along the main line and mark the reference dots. Keep moving your template and marking all the reference dots. In this example we need twelve blocks in a three by four grid.

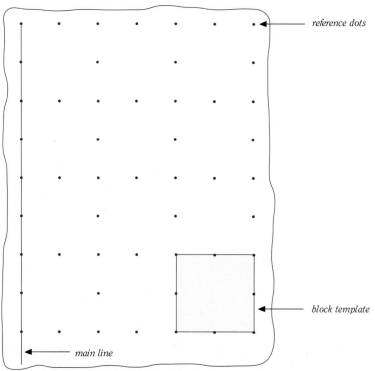

reference dots

block template

main line

Use the block template to mark your reference dots.

Next, using your removable marker and a straight edge, connect the reference dots to create the **main lines** of your block design. Unless your design is straight lines that you plan to quilt using masking tape as a guide (see page 10), place your background fabric (with the basic blocks marked) on the working pattern on the lightbox and trace the motifs.

Once you have the top marked, add borders if you are using them (see page 19). Layer, baste, and quilt (see page 19 – 20). After quilting, remove all marks according to the directions that come with your brand of removable marker. Bind and add your design elements.

In the Yo-Yo Pinwheel quilt, I used tiny yo-yos as my design elements. The finished yo-yos were stitched like buttons to the already quilted piece.

Main quilting lines are marked, cross-hatch motifs being added.

QUILT SECOND

Begin as you did in Quilt First by cutting and pressing your background fabric and drawing a main line at least one inch in from the edge of one side. Place your template on the main line as before and mark your reference dots first with removable marker (the purple air-erasable one is nice here), then mark them with thread dots (little thread back stitches).

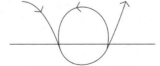

Making a thread dot

Because you have to press your appliqué, embroidery, or paint before you quilt, any marking pen needs to be removed after the surface design is applied. In order to keep your reference marks in place through the first process, they need to be made with thread. Use a pale color, so as not to risk any color-bleed when removing other markings and pressing.

Use the thread dots to align your background fabric over your working pattern on the lightbox. Mark your applied design. (In this example we're using appliqué and embroidery similar to that of the single Pinwheel block on pages 80-81.) Remove from the lightbox and create your designs on the fabric using your chosen technique (appliqué, embroidery, painting, etc.). Remove all marks using the directions that come with your brand of removable marker. Leave the thread dots and press the quilt top.

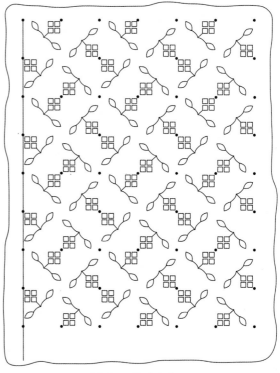

Mark applied design

Using the thread dots for reference, mark your main quilt lines as before with a removable marker and a ruler. Return the quilt top to the working pattern on the lightbox and mark any secondary lines or motifs needed for quilting.

Add borders if you are using them (see page 19). Layer, baste, and quilt (see page 19 – 20). After quilting, remove all marks including the thread dots. Bind your quilt to finish (see page 20).

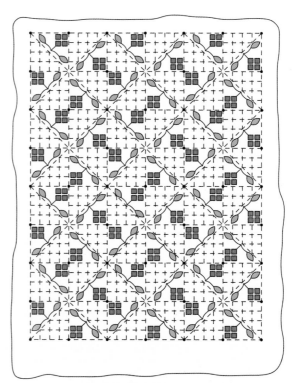

Mark quilting lines

18

BORDERS

A border or two can add a lot to a quilted design. These should be added before you quilt. If you are using the Quilt First method, add the borders after you have the quilting pattern marked. If you are doing Quilt Second, add the borders after you have applied your surface design (appliqué, embroidery, paint, etc.). Cut the borders the desired width and measure your piece for the correct length. Using a $1/4''$ inch seam, sew the side borders on first and then the top and bottom. Repeat this same order for any additional borders.

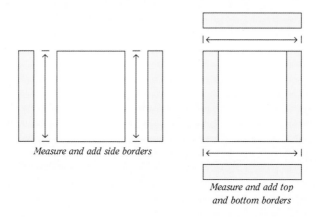

Measure and add side borders

Measure and add top and bottom borders

QUILTING

To hand quilt or machine quilt? This is a question answered by your own passion. I am an avid hand quilter. The quiet, relaxed style suits me. The easy-to-pick-up and simple-to-stitch work invites me to create unrestricted designs and patterns. And I very much like the appearance of hand quilting.

However, if the machine muse has you snagged, translate my creations to fit your favored method. You basically need to keep your work taut and have a plan of action. I would begin by stitching all the main lines of the blocks with as few stops and starts as possible. Interior designs would benefit from continuous line patterns.

Whether by hand or by machine, it is important to prepare your layers for quilting. I lap quilt (no hoop or frame), and I find it works well for small, wall-hanging size quilts. I have also been successful with full-size quilts using this method.

Cut your batting and backing material at least 1" larger than your quilt top all around. Lay out the backing wrong-side up, then place the batting on top, and finally, add the top right-side up. Baste the layers together with long stitches using white thread. Baste in a grid with lines up and down and side-to-side about four inches apart. This basting will keep all the layers together as you quilt.

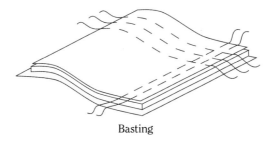

Basting

The quilting stitch is a simple running stitch that goes through all three layers of fabric. Use an 18"-long piece of quilting thread. Tie a knot, pull it between the layers (inside the batting) and begin quilting. To end a thread, make a knot close to the quilt top and pull it into the batting. Let the needle travel between the layers for an inch or so, then come up and snip.

Quilting stitch

Begin by quilting the main quilt lines that define the blocks. Then go back and quilt the designs you have chosen for the quilted pieces. You may remove the basting as you go or after the quilting is completed. Trim the outer edges even. I usually allow 1/2" beyond the outermost line of quilting that defines the blocks, and stitch my binding on just outside or on that line of quilting

BINDING

The binding is the finished edge of your quilt and serves as a frame to accent the finished design. Choose a color that brings out the favorite or main color in the design. I lay several different choices along the side of the quilt to help envision my favorite.

Fabric grain

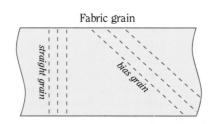

straight grain   *bias grain*

Adding bindings

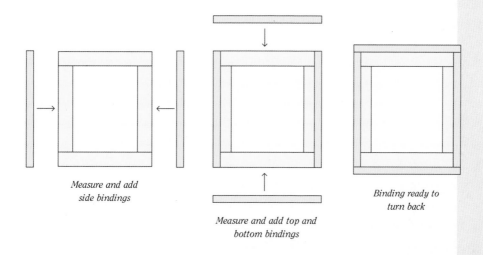

*Measure and add
side bindings*

*Measure and add top and
bottom bindings*

*Binding ready to
turn back*

Binding corners

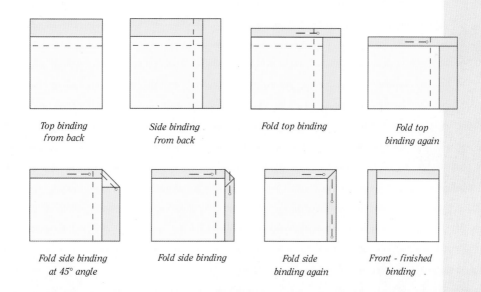

*Top binding
from back*

*Side binding
from back*

Fold top binding

*Fold top
binding again*

*Fold side binding
at 45° angle*

Fold side binding

*Fold side
binding again*

*Front - finished
binding*

Most of my quilts are square or rectangular so single-fold straight-grain binding serves well. If your piece has a curved outer edge, you will need bias-cut binding. Use a rotary cutter, ruler, and mat, to cut the strips two-inches wide, selvedge to selvedge. Sew the binding first on the sides and then the top and bottom, using a 1/2" seam or following the last line of quilting. Turn the binding to the back and fold the raw edge under about 1/2". Fold the binding once more and blind stitch it down being careful not to let any stitches go through to the front. I pin the entire binding in place before stitching it on the back.

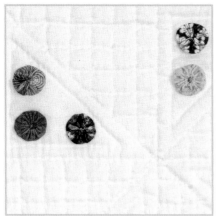
Yo-Yo Pinwheel, page 24

Lacy Log Cabin, page 28

Shoo-Fly, page 32

Grandmother's Little Angels, page 36

Lonestar, page 42

Attic Windows, page 46

Cross Variation, page 50

Storm at Sea, page 54

Bow Ties, page 58

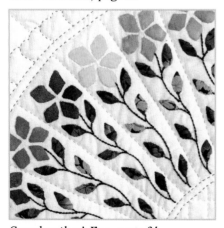
Grandmother's Fan, page 64

Churn Dash, page 68

Maple Leaves, page 72

Projects

Single Appliqué Blocks, pages 78-91

Yo-Yo Pinwheel

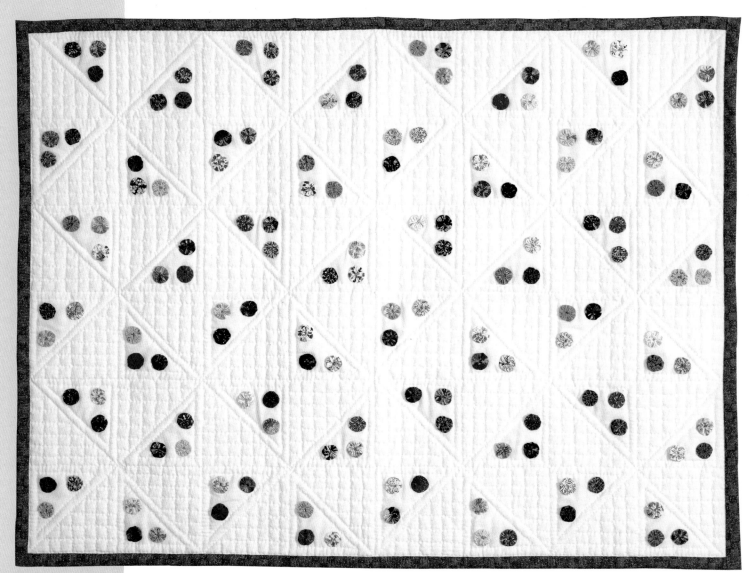

29" x 22", a "Quilt First" project

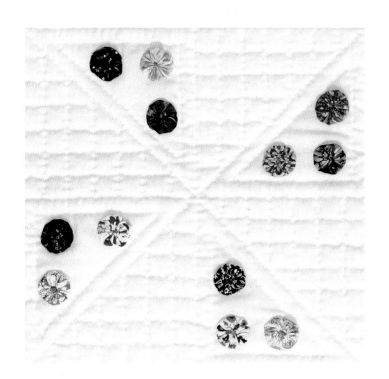

This project is pure fun. The simple yet classic block is called Pinwheel. With all straight lines to quilt, this version of a basic Four-Patch design is a good project for beginners. From the scrap bag come bits of many fabrics to create the simple decoration, gathered circles, which are fondly called yo-yos.

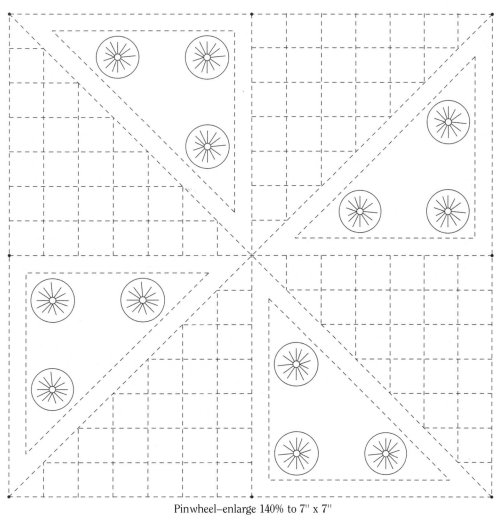

Pinwheel–enlarge 140% to 7" x 7"

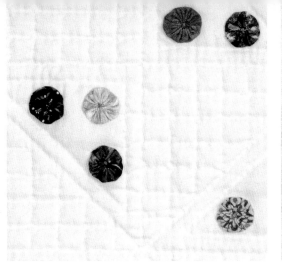
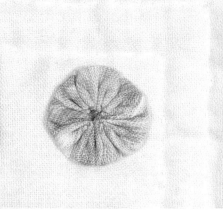

Materials

Background muslin 31" x 24"

Batting and Backing 33" x 26"

7" x 7" Block Template

Full-size working pattern for block

Natural color quilting thread

Binding 3/8 yard, cut four strips 2"-wide straight grain

144 little yo-yos from scraps

Directions

Spray starch the background fabric. Using a removable marker, draw the main line one inch from one long side of your background fabric. Using the 7" x 7" block template, mark the reference dots in removable marker for a grid of three blocks by four blocks. With the same marker and a straight edge, connect the dots to form the main blocks. Then, using your working pattern and the lightbox, mark the inside quilting lines with a removable marker.

Baste the three layers (top, batting, and backing) together for quilting (see page 19) and quilt the marked design (see page 20). Remove all marks and basting threads. Trim the outer edges 1/2" from the last line of quilting. Bind (see page 20).

Yo-Yos

You will need 144 yo-yos. Stitch three yo-yos to each open triangle.

To make a yo-yo, cut a 1½" circle of fabric. Turn under a small, even allowance and run a gathering thread around the edges. Gather the circle and secure the thread with a few tiny stitches. Sew onto the quilt as you would a button, stitching through all three layers.

Lacy Log Cabin

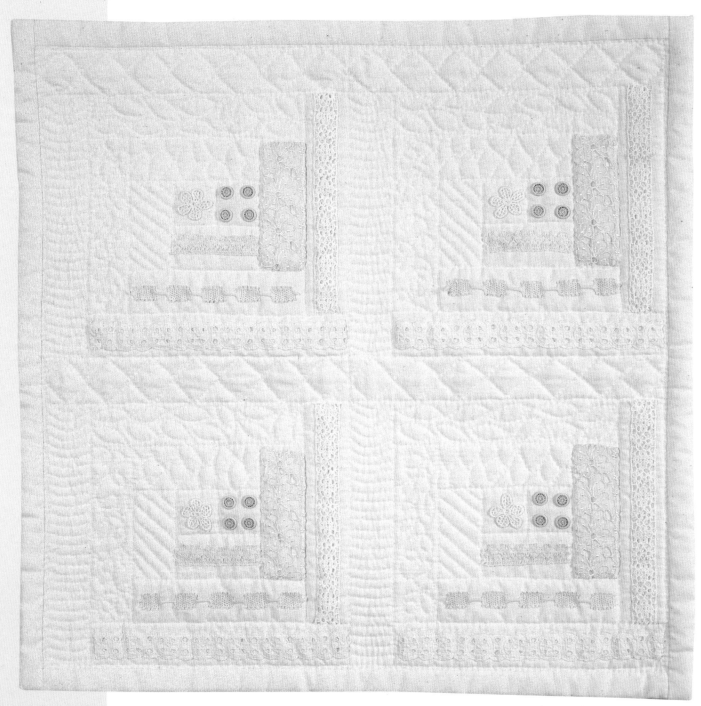

18½" x 18½", a "Quilt First" project

Traditionally sewn with light and dark fabrics, I've adapted this old-fashioned quilt block to quilting and lace to form the "logs" of the cabin. Those bits of frills and old buttons you have been saving will find the right home in this easy-to-stitch project.

Lacy Log Cabin–enlarge 150% to 8³/₄" x 8³/₄"

Materials

Background muslin 21" x 21"

Batting and Backing 23" x 23"

8¾" x 8¾" Block Template (for corners only)

Full-size working pattern for block

Natural color quilting thread

Binding ⅛ yard, cut two strips 2"-wide straight grain

Scraps of laces, old buttons to fit the block strips.
(They may be narrower.)

Thread to match lace

Directions

Spray starch the background fabric. Using a removable marker, draw your main line one inch from one side. Using your block template, mark only the corner dots for each block. Because the inner lines of this block are not symmetrical, it is confusing to use more dots for reference. With your removable marker and ruler, mark the outside lines of the blocks. Then, using your working pattern and the lightbox, mark the quilting lines and designs. Pay attention that you keep the block design in the same position for each block unless you choose a different Log Cabin block arrangement.

Baste the three layers (top, batting, and backing) together for quilting (see page 19). Quilt the marked design (see page 20). Remove all marks and basting threads. Trim the outer edges ½" from the last line of quilting. Bind (see page 20).

Select the laces for each "log" section. Cut four of each selection; one for each block. Cut them the length of the section plus ½" for a ¼" turn-under on each end. With thread to match the lace, stitch the lace pieces through the top and batting only, hiding your stitches in the lace as needed. I selected four tiny buttons for the center square and sewed them through all three layers.

QUILT
1st

Shoo-Fly

19" x 19", a "Quilt First" project

A Nine-Patch design updated with crisp lines and bold dashes of color, this design is created with quilt lines drawing the "patches" and highlighted with a single square of paper-foundation piecing in each block. This popular piecing technique is a great project to try your hand at.

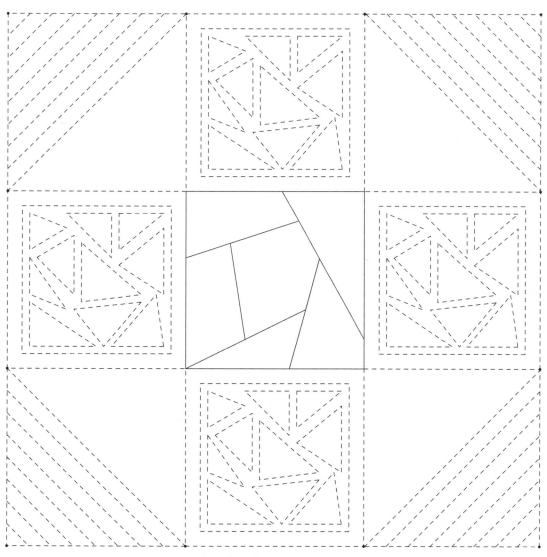

Shoo-Fly—enlarge 160% to 9" x 9"

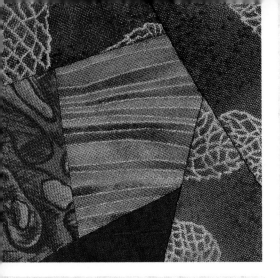

Materials

Background muslin 21" x 21"

Batting and Backing 23" x 23"

9" x 9" Block Template

Full-size working pattern for block

Natural color quilting thread

Binding ⅛ yard, cut two strips 2"-wide straight grain

Light-weight paper for foundation

Black marker

Scraps of fabrics for paper-foundation squares

Thread to match paper-foundation squares

Directions

Spray starch the background fabric. Using a removable marker, mark the main line one inch from one side. Using the 9" x 9" block template, mark the reference dots in removable marker for a four block design. With the same marker and a straight edge, connect the dots to form the basic Nine-Patch blocks. Then, using the working pattern and the lightbox, mark the quilting lines with a removable marker.

Baste the three layers (top, batting, and backing) together for quilting (see page 19). Quilt the marked design (see page 20). Remove all marks and basting threads. Trim the outer edges ½" from the last line of quilting. Bind (see page 20).

Appliqué the paper foundation squares to the center square of each block. Turn under the raw edges so that they are just inside the quilting lines that define the center square and appliqué (see page 14). Catch only the top fabric and a bit of the batting with the appliqué stitches.

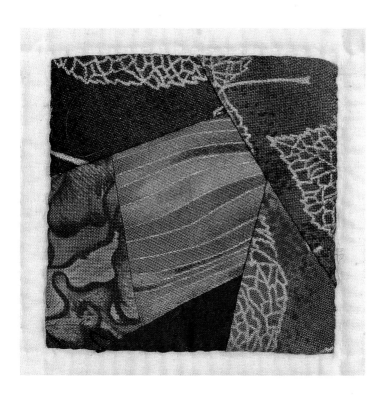

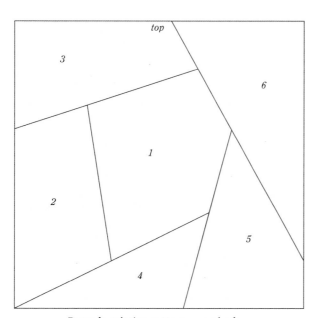

Paper foundation pattern — make four.

Paper-Foundation Squares

Make four copies of the foundation design on light-weight paper. I use a dark marker so that I can see the design on both sides of the paper. I also write "top" on the right side as a reminder to keep all four blocks the same.

Cut four of each piece—one through six. Make them with generous seam allowances, at least 1/2" larger than the drawn size.

Pin (or use a bit of glue stick) the number one piece right-side up in its place on the top side of the paper pattern with allowances covering the drawn lines. Holding it up to a light or lightbox makes this placement easy.

Take piece number two and position it on the paper pattern with the seam allowances covering the drawn lines. Then flip it over onto piece number one, and with right-sides together, line up their common seam. Pin in place and turn the paper over. By hand or machine, stitch this line. You are sewing from the back through all layers. The line you can see through the paper is your guide. Cut the threads and return to the front of the paper. Flip piece number two back and finger press flat.

Continue in this manner, one piece at a time, in the order marked. Finish one through six for each of the four squares. Press well and tear out the paper carefully. This will give you four identical squares.

QUILT
1st

Grandmother's Little Angels (Grandmother's Flower Garden)

18" x 18", a "Quilt First" project

My little Snippet Angels have gathered in Grandmother's Flower Garden, one of the names given to this hexagon pattern quilt. What a darling piece for that little girl's room, or for any angel collector. A bit of whimsey is good for the heart.

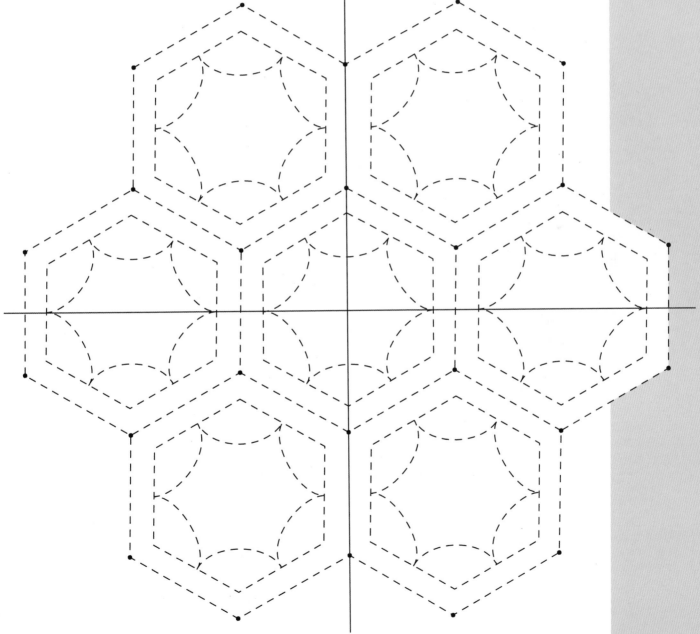

Grandmother's Little Angels

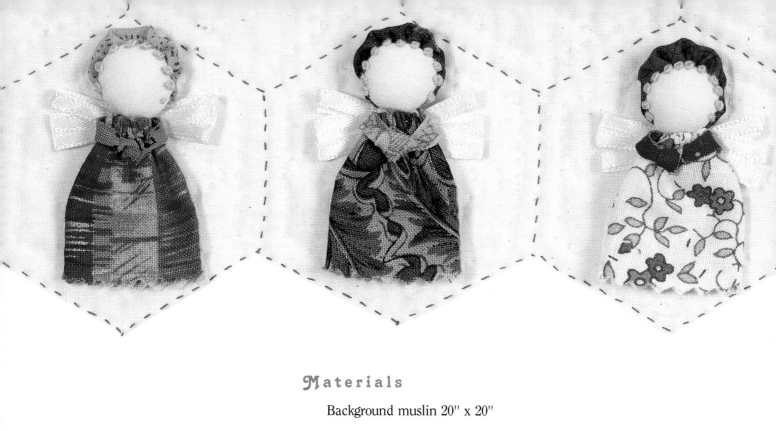

Materials

Background muslin 20" x 20"

Batting and Backing 22" x 22"

Full-size working pattern for the entire design

Quilting threads in yellow, light blue, and medium green

Binding ⅛ yard, cut two strips 2"-wide straight grain

Directions for Quilt

Spray starch the background fabric. It is easiest to work from a complete full-size pattern for this design. You will need 20" x 20" paper. I usually tape some smaller sheets together. Draw a center line up and down and side to side. (You can fold the paper to find these lines). Use a lightbox and trace the seven hexagon pattern (see page 37) onto your paper, lining up the center lines (solid lines) on the pattern.

Moving the hexagon pattern, place and trace the design to create the configuration in the photo. Echo the large center motif with a line 1/4" all around. There is no need to draw the random shell pattern unless you are more comfortable having this marked. The shells are not all the same size and are created by quilting around a layer at a time. Once you have the paper pattern drawn, trace this design onto the muslin background with a removable marker. Again—only draw the random shells necessary. Once you have quilted a few shells you will find this design is easy, fun, and quick to quilt.

Baste the three layers (top, batting, and backing) together for quilting (see page 19). Quilt the marked design (see page 20). Remove all marks and basting threads. Square up the piece. Bind (see page 20).

Pin or stitch the Snippet Angels onto the hexagons, referring to the photo for placement.

Color for Quilting

Medium-green	hexagon outlines
Yellow	inside hexagon lines and star shapes
Light-Blue	random shells

Material for 21 Angels

Scraps of fabrics

Round toothpicks

Fabric glue

Bit of stuffing for heads

Ribbon for wings

Floss for hair

Snippet Angels

The Head

Cut a 1¼" circle of muslin. Gather the circle. Add a small bit
of stuffing, then close the gathered hole. Secure the thread
with several backstitches.

Snip a round toothpick in half and push the pointed end through the
gathered hole and out the top edge of the head. Snip off the point. Put a bit
of glue on the top of the toothpick and pull back into the head.

The Dress

Cut two 1½" square pieces of fabric. (You may use pinking shears if you have them.) With
right sides together, sew ⅛" side seams. Turn right side out. Tuck under a tiny hem at
the top edge and run a gathering thread around. With a little glue on the angel's neck,
gather the dress around the neck and secure with a few backstitches. Cover the entire
neck with the dress.

The Arms

Cut a ⅜" strip of fabric on the bias, about two inches long. Fold in half lengthwise and
use a little glue to secure the folded piece. Tie a knot in the middle. Trim the arms to
about ½" from the knot. With a dab of glue on each arm end, attach the arms to the
dress at the sides and slightly to the back. Put the folded edge up.

The Hair

Make a row of French knots along the edge of the head or add a bit of wool or curly threads.

The Halo

Cut a 1½" circle and gather into a yo-yo. Glue to the back of the head with the gathered side towards the back of the head. Keep the bottom of the halo even with the neck.

The Wings

Wind a small length of narrow ribbon in several loops and secure the center by tying or
sewing stitches to form a bow. Make wings about 1¼" wide. Use a bit of lace or cut a
wing from decorative paper, if you like, to finish your angel. Glue the wings to the angel's
back just below the halo.

Lonestar

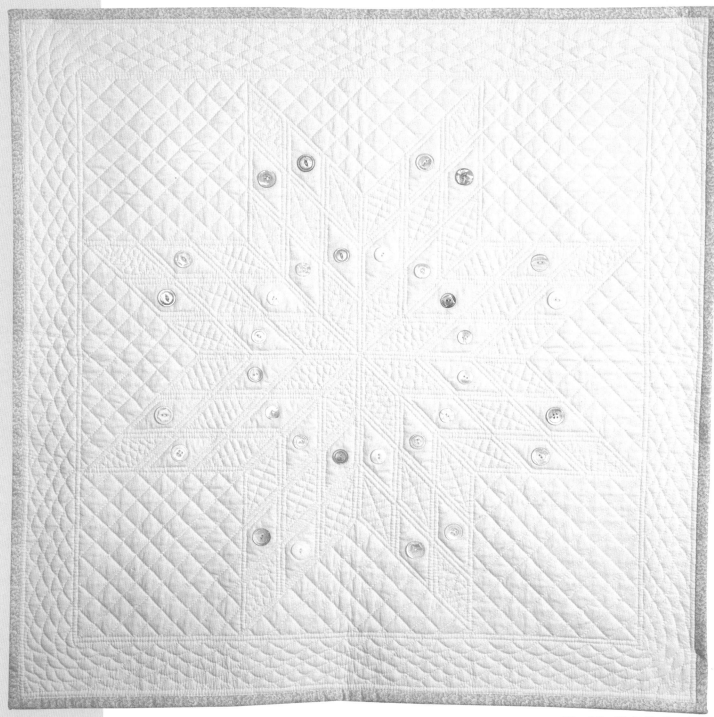

34" x 34", a "Quilt First" project

A grand design is the Lone Star, also called the Star of Bethlehem. Quilted diamonds form an eight pointed star that can stand on its own as a whole-cloth quilt, but a soft patterned binding and a few shell buttons make it a radiant design.

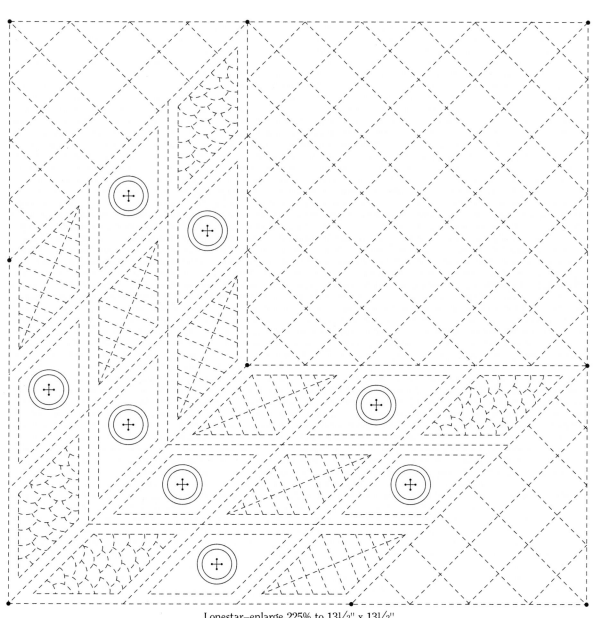

Lonestar–enlarge 225% to 13½" x 13½"

Materials

Background muslin 36" x 36"

Batting and Backing 38" x 38"

¼ of the full-size working pattern

Natural color quilting thread

Binding, ⅜ yard, cut four strips 2"-wide straight grain

32 shell buttons (approx. 1 ½" diameter)

Directions

Spray starch the background fabric. It is easiest to work from ¼ of the full-size working pattern, as Lonestar is not a block design. With paper 19" x 19" and using the diamond segment pattern (see page 43) you can create your quarter pattern. Refer to the graphic for placement.

Fold the background fabric in half both ways and lightly press to create centerlines. Then, using your one-quarter pattern and the lightbox, trace the quiltlines with a removable marker. To prevent the pattern from shifting while marking, use a few pins to secure. Continue and mark the other three quarters of the top. Take it slowly, as this is a large piece to mark. There is no need to draw the random shell border pattern unless you are more comfortable having this marked. The shells are not all the same size and are created by quilting around a row at a time.

Baste the three layers (top, batting, and backing) together for quilting (see page 19). Quilt the marked design (see page 20) and then the random shell border pattern. Remove all marks and basting threads. Trim the outer edge ½" from the last line of quilting. Bind (see page 20).

Stitch the buttons to the unquilted diamonds through all three layers.

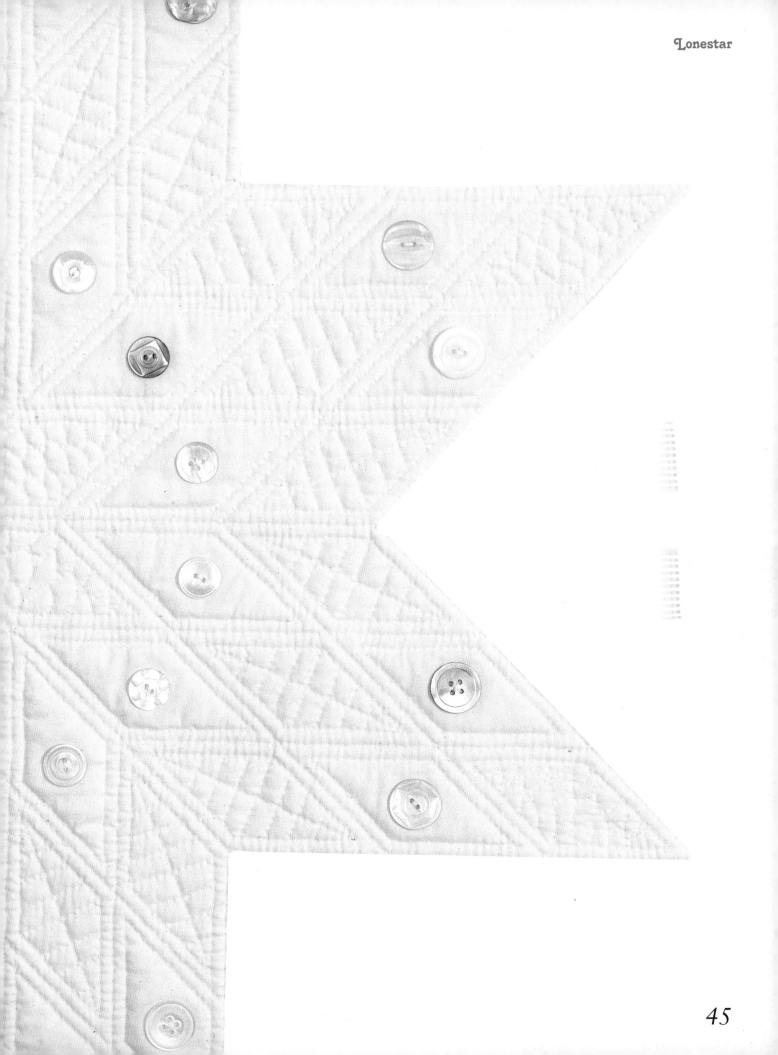

QUILT
1st

Attic Windows

Cover photography by Sue Leaf

25" x 31", a "Quilt First" project

There are flowers on view from my attic windows. Appliquéd squares of muslin with transferred photos fill each pane. You could also use pictures of children, of friends, of any photographed time. A wonderful idea for a memory quilt!

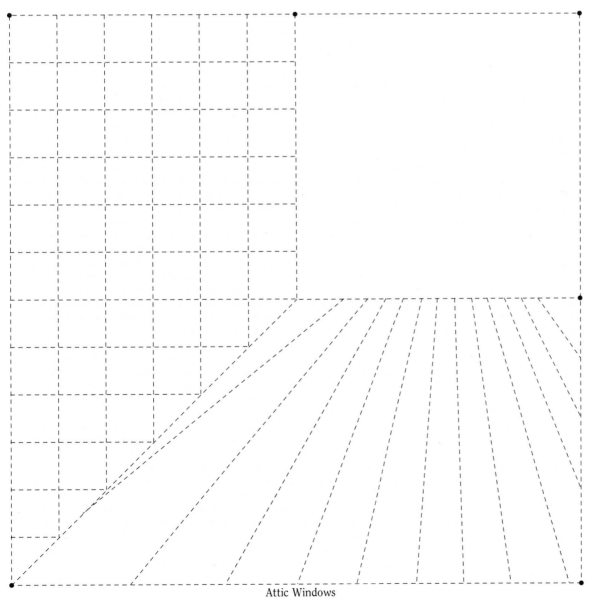

Attic Windows

Materials

Background muslin 27" x 33"

Batting and Backing 29" x 35"

6" x 6" Block Template

Full-size working pattern for block

Natural color quilting thread

Binding ⅜ yard, cut four strips 2"-wide straight grain

30 photo transfer items (3"-square plus ¼" turn under all around)

Thread to match photo transfer items

Directions

Spray starch the background fabric. Using a removable marker, draw your main line one inch from one long side. Using the 6" x 6" block template and the removable marker, mark the dots for a four block by five block grid. With the same marker and a straight edge, connect the dots for the 6" x 6" blocks. Then, using your working pattern and the light-box, mark the quilting lines with a removable marker.

Baste the three layers (top, batting, and backing) together for quilting (see page 19). Quilt the marked design (see page 20). Remove all marks and basting threads. Trim the outer edges ½" from the last line of quilting. Bind (see page 20).

Appliqué your photo transfer squares onto the "windows," stitching through the top and a bit of the batting with an appliqué stitch (see page 14).

Photo Transfer

There are many photo transfer papers and fabrics available. I had my photos directly transferred onto muslin on a machine at one of my favorite quilt shops. Ask at your craft or quilt shop for the options available.

49

QUILT
1st

Cross Variation

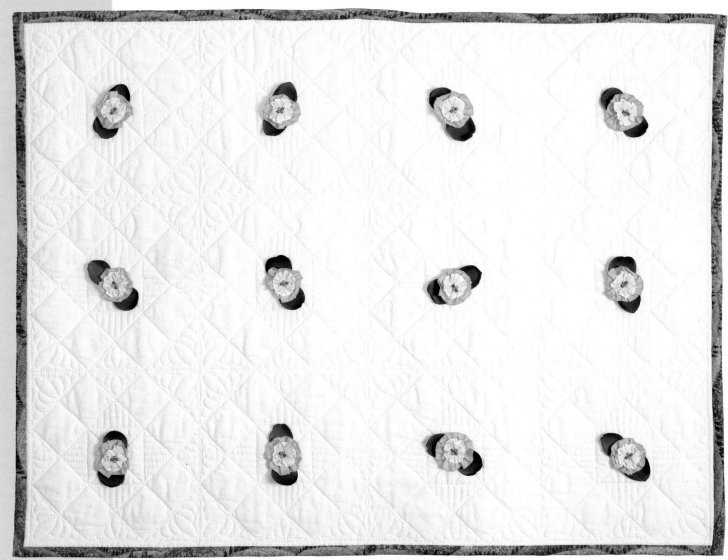

37" x 28", a "Quilt First" project

Elegant ribbon flowers adorn this richly quilted design. A dozen blocks—each with a single bloom at their center that can easily change to another color or style if you attach them with a pin or velcro. Ribbon flowers are great fun to make and this is an excellent way to display this craft.

Cross Variation–enlarge 163% to 9" x 9"

Materials

Background Muslin 39" x 30"

Batting and backing 41" x 32"

9" x 9" Block Template

Full size working pattern for block

Natural color quilting thread

Binding ⅜ yard, cut four strips 2"-wide straight grain

12 ribbon flowers

Directions

Spray starch the background fabric. Using a removable marker, draw your main line one inch from one long side. Using your block template and the removable marker, mark dots for a three block by four block grid. With the same marker and a straight edge, connect the dots for the 9" x 9" blocks. Then, using your working pattern and the lightbox, mark the quilting lines with a removable marker.

Baste the three layers (top, batting, and backing) together for quilting (see page 19). Quilt the marked design (see page 20). Remove all marks and basting threads. Trim the outer edges ½" from the last line of quilting. Bind (see page 20).

Velcro, pin, or stitch the ribbon flowers to the quilt, referring to the photo for placement.

Ribbon Flowers

12 lengths of $1\frac{1}{2}$"-wide wired ribbon—cut to $8\frac{1}{2}$" long

24 leaves

12 velcro dots

48 4mm beads

Ribbon Flower

Stitch the ends of each length of wired ribbon together (a French seam is best), to form a ring. Run a strong thread in a gathering stitch around the ring $\frac{1}{3}$ in from the lighter color side of the ribbon. Pull the gathers together to form a rosette. Secure the thread. Shape the flower by bending the wires. Stitch four 4mm glass beads into each center. I glued the two pre-made leaves to the back of the flower with fabric glue. If you wish, add a self-sticking velcro dot to the back of the flowers with its other half to the quilt.

Storm At Sea

16½" x 16½", a "Quilt Second" project

Redwork roses are a relaxing pastime for quilters. The embroidery is highlighted by simple straight-line quilting. Give this one a try.

Storm At Sea–enlarge 288% to 15$\frac{1}{2}$" x 15$\frac{1}{2}$"

55

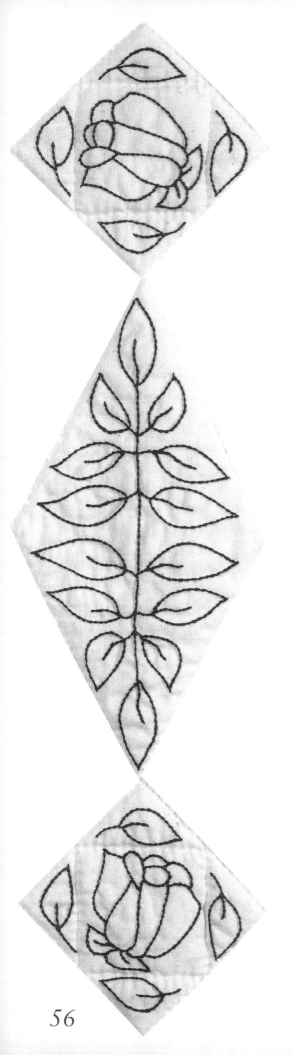

Materials

Background muslin 18" x 18"

Batting and Backing 20" x 20"

Full-size working pattern for the entire design

Natural color quilting thread

Two skeins embroidery floss, Turkey red

Pale color thread for reference dots

Binding 1/8 yard, cut two strips 2"-wide straight grain

Directions

Spray starch the background fabric. It is easiest to work from a complete full-size pattern for this design. Draw this on 18" x 18" paper using the pattern provided. Darken the dots on the pattern. Then, using your working pattern and lightbox, trace only the dots and the embroidery designs onto the background fabric. To prevent the pattern from shifting while marking, use a few pins to secure.

Mark the dots with thread (see page 17). Embroider the red-work roses using two strands of floss and a stem or outline stitch. Remove all the marks. Leave the thread dots. Using a medium-heat steam iron, press the embroidered piece well and carefully. Do not pull or warp the fabric.

Lay the pressed top back over the full-size pattern, aligning the thread dots with the dots on the pattern. A few pins at the dots helps hold things as you go.

With a removable marker and the lightbox, mark all the quilting lines. Remove the top from the pattern.

Baste the three layers (top, batting, and backing) together for quilting (see page 19). Quilt the marked design (see page 20). Remove all marks, thread dots, and basting threads. Trim the outer edge 1/2" from the last line of quilting. Bind (see page 20).

QUILT
2nd

Bow Tie, in three versions
Appliqué, Fabric-Painted, and Redwork

9" x 9", a "Quilt Second" project

10" x 16", a "Quilt Second" project

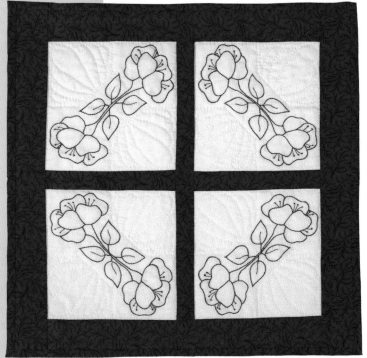

17" x 17", a "Quilt Second" project

This simple block is shown in three different surface techniques: appliqué, fabric paints, and redwork embroidery. And in three different arrangements: a two block design, a single block design, and a four block set with sashing design. These small projects give you a chance to play!

Bow Tie

Materials

Applique Version

Background muslin 8" x 14"

Batting and Backing 14" x 20"

Full-size working pattern for block

Natural color quilting thread

Two blue fabrics for flowers

One green for leaves and stems

Embroidery floss in white, green, and yellow

Border ⅛ yard, cut two strips 2½"-wide straight grain

Binding ⅛ yard, cut two strips 2"-wide straight grain

Painted Version

Background muslin 8" x 8"

Batting and Backing 11" x 11"

Full-size working pattern for block

Green quilting thread

Acrylic fabric paint in yellow and green

Permanent pens in black and red

Border ⅛ yard, cut one strip 2"-wide straight grain

Facing fabric 9½" x 9½"

Redwork Version

Background muslin ⅜ yard, cut four squares 8" x 8"

Batting and Backing 20" x 20"

Full-size working pattern for block

Natural color quilting thread

Embroidery floss in turkey red

Sashing ⅛ yard, cut one strip 1½"-wide straight grain

Border ¼ yard, cut two strips 2½"-wide straight grain

Binding ⅛ yard, cut two strips 2"-wide straight grain

Directions

Appliqué Version

Spray starch the background fabric. Using your working pattern and the lightbox, trace only the reference dots and appliqué design onto the background. Allow at least 1" in from the edges all around. Place one block next to the other. Mark the dots with thread (see page 17). Appliqué the flowers, referring to the pattern for appliqué order. Embroider the stamens and leaf stems. Remove any marks. Leave the thread dots. With a medium-heat iron, press carefully from the back to avoid warping the fabric. With a rotary cutter, ruler, and mat, trim the appliquéd background ¼" from the dots. This allows a ¼" seam allowance for attaching the borders.

Sew on the blue border (see page 19). Press the entire top.

Lay the pressed top back over the full-size working pattern, aligning the thread dots with the dots on the pattern. A few pins at the dots helps hold things as you go.

With a removable marker, mark all the quilting lines.

Baste the three layers (top, batting, and backing) together for quilting (see page 19). Quilt the marked design, around the appliqué, and ¼" in on the sides of the border (see page 20). Remove all marks, thread dots, and basting threads. Bind (see page 20).

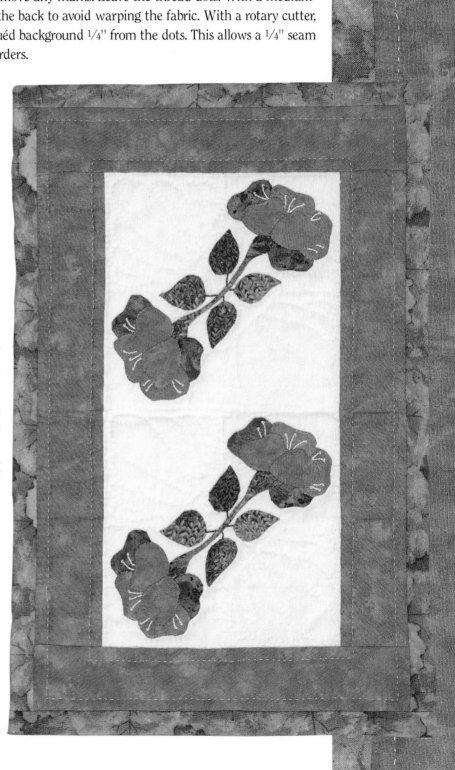

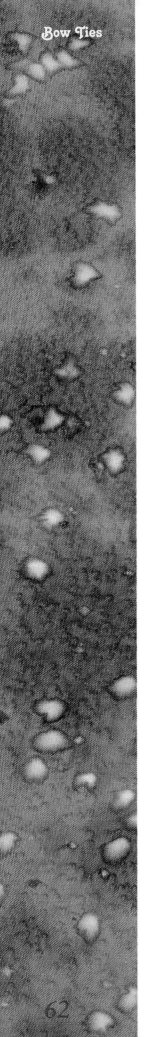

Directions

Fabric-Painted Version

Do not spray starch the fabric as it may interfere with the paint adhesion.

Using your working pattern and the lightbox, mark the reference dots with a removable marker. Allow at least 1" in from the edges all around. Mark the painted design with permanent marker (a Pigma® pen is good). Mark the dots with thread. Remove the dot marks with a damp cloth.

Paint the design with the fabric paints (see page 14). Allow the paint to dry. Add the details with the permanent pens. Set the paint according to the directions on the paint container.

Trim the block ¼" away from the dots. Using ¼" seam, add the borders (see page 19). Press. Lay the pressed top back over the working pattern, aligning the dots and painted design. With the removable marker, mark all the quilting lines.

Baste the three layers (top, batting, and backing) together for quilting (see page 19). Quilt the marked design, around the painted flowers, and ¼" in on the sides of the border (see page 20). Remove all marks, thread dots, and basting threads.

With right sides together, pin the top and facing on all four sides. Using a ¼" seam, sew three of the sides together. Turn right side out. Hand stitch the fourth side closed.

Redwork Version

Spray starch the background squares. Using your working pattern and the lightbox, mark the dots and embroidery design on each of the four background squares with removable marker. Mark the dots with thread. Using two strands of Turkey red floss, stem stitch each block. Add a French knot at the end of each stamen. Remove any marks and leave the thread dots. Press. Trim the blocks 1/4" away from the dots. Assemble blocks with sashing and borders (see page 19).

Follow directions for marking, quilting, and binding as with the appliquéd version.

Grandmother's Fan

28" x 19", a "Quilt Second" project

A burst of color! Colors in the order of the rainbow decorate each quilted fan with eight long-stem flowers. More color is added by the use of many different colors of quilting thread. A stunning mix of quilting and appliqué.

Grandmother's Fan—enlarge 160% to 9" x 9"

Materials

Background muslin 30" x 21"

Batting and Backing 32" x 23"

9" x 9" Block Template

Full-size working pattern for block

Quilting threads in yellow, light blue, red, green, and orange

Binding ⅜ yard, cut three strips 2"-wide straight grain

Rainbow color fabrics for flowers

Green fabric for leaves

Embroidery floss in green for stems

Thread to match appliqué fabrics

Directions

Spray starch the background fabric. Using a removable marker, draw your main line 1" in from one long side. Using the 9" x 9" block template and the removable marker, mark the reference dots for a two block by three block grid. Mark the dots with thread.

Using the corner dots to align, place the background fabric over the working pattern and trace only the appliqué and embroidery designs for each block. Use the removable marker.

Appliqué the flowers, referring to the photo for color placement (see page 14). Embroider the stems in green using two strands of floss for a stem or outline stitch. Remove all the marks. Leave the thread dots. Press the appliquéd top. This piece has a lot of appliqué, so press as evenly as you can.

Lay the blocks over the working pattern using the thread dots and the appliqué as a guide. Pin where necessary to the pattern to keep things in place. Mark the quilting lines with a removable marker. Adjust where necessary if the appliqué has drawn the fabric a bit. Little changes are not noticeable. Remove the top from the pattern.

Baste the three layers (top, batting, and backing) together for quilting (see page 19). Quilt the marked design (see page 20). Remove all marks, thread dots, and basting threads. Trim the outer edge ½" from the last line of quilting. Bind (see page 20).

Color for Quilting

Orange   the main block lines

Yellow   inner circle crosshatching

Red   inner circle double line, top of the fan hearts

Blue   between the fan blades, radiating lines at the fan top

Green   double line at the top of the fan

Churn Dash

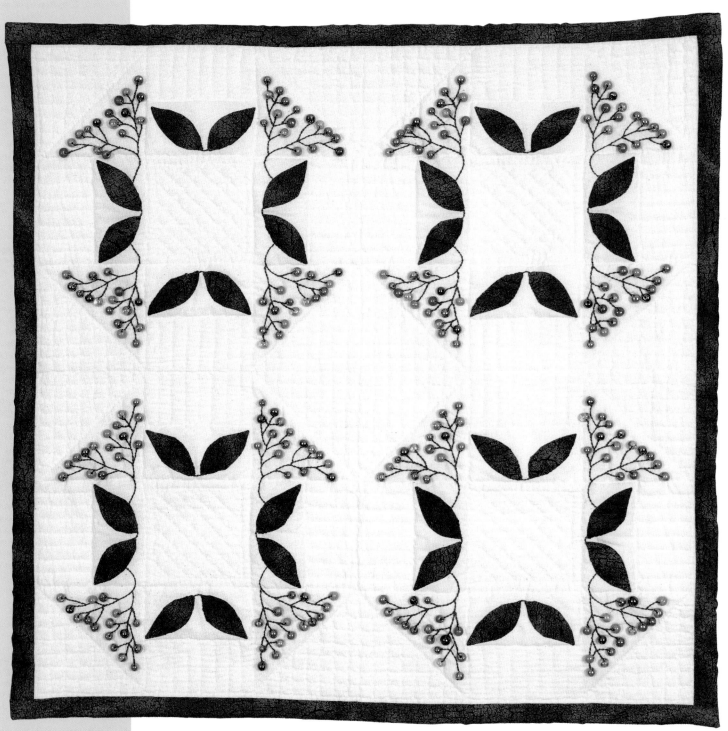

19" x 19", a "Quilt Second" project

The glow of iridescent glass beads gives this take on a standard quilt block a special feel. The appliqué is simply leaves and embroidered stems ending with beads. You'll love the texture and feel of this project.

Churn Dash–enlarge 160% to 9" x 9"

Materials

Background muslin 21" x 21"

Batting and Backing 23" x 23"

9" x 9" Block Template

Full-size working pattern for block

Natural color quilting thread

Thread to match appliqué fabrics

Binding ⅛ yard, cut two strips 2"-wide straight grain

Green fabric for leaves

Embroidery floss in green

256 (6mm) glass beads

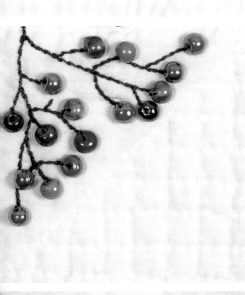

Directions

Spray starch the background fabric. Using a removable marker and the lightbox, place the background fabric over the working pattern and trace only the reference dots, appliqué, and embroidery designs for each block. Mark the dots with thread.

Appliqué the leaves (see page 14). Embroider the stems using two strands of green floss and a stem stitch. Remove all the marks. Leave the thread dots. Press the appliquéd top.

Lay the blocks over the working pattern using the dots and the appliqué as a guide. Pin where necessary to the pattern to keep things in place. Mark the quilting lines with a removable marker.

Baste the three layers (top, batting, and backing) together for quilting (see page 19). Quilt the marked design (see page 20). Remove all marks, thread dots, and basting threads. Trim the outer edge ½" from the last line of quilting. Bind (see page 20).

Use double quilting thread to stitch the beads to the ends of the stems. Stitch through all three layers to keep these heavy items stable.

QUILT
2nd

Maple Leaves

29" x 29", a "Quilt Second" project

A pieced project. The Maple Leaf blocks are first appliquéd and then pieced on-point. Adding corner triangles creates the square, and quilting creates the magic. A challenging project.

Corner triangles–enlarge 235% to 18" on the longest (diagonal) side–add ¼" seam all around

Maple Leaves–enlarge 143% to 9" x 9"

Materials

Background muslin ¾ yard, cut four squares 11" x 11"

Cut four triangles, measure after sewing together the four appliqué blocks. The triangles should be cut from two 13½" blocks, cut once on the diagonal.

Batting and Backing 32" x 32"

Full-size working pattern for block

Full-size working pattern for corner triangle

Natural color quilting thread

Thread to match appliqué fabrics

Green embroidery floss for stems

Binding ⅜ yard, cut four strips 2"-wide straight grain

Border ⅜ yard, cut four strips 2"-wide straight grain
Measure for length after piecing center

Green fabrics for leaves and seeds

Directions

Spray starch the four 11" x 11" blocks for appliqué. Using a removable marker and the lightbox, place each 11" x 11" piece of fabric over the working pattern leaving one inch all around. First mark the reference dots and the appliqué design in removable marker. Mark the dots with thread.

Appliqué the leaves and seeds (see page 14). Follow the order of the appliqué on the pattern. Embroider the stems using two strands of green embroidery floss and a stem stitch. Remove all marks but leave the thread dots. With a medium-heat iron, press well from the back. Try to keep the block square. Make four appliquéd leaf blocks.

With a rotary cutter, ruler, and mat, trim the appliquéd blocks ¼" from the dots, keeping them square. Using a ¼" seam allowance, sew the four blocks together to form a larger square. Try to just miss including the thread dots in the seam if you can. Press.

Attach the four corner triangles using ¼" seams. Press. Add the borders (see page 19). Press the entire top.

Returning to the lightbox, align each block over the working pattern and mark the quilting lines for the blocks and the corner triangles with a removable marker.

Baste the three layers (top, batting, and backing) together for quilting (see page 19). Quilt the marked designs as well as along the block seams and around the leaves and seeds (see page 20). Remove all marks, thread dots, and basting threads. Trim the outer edges ½" from the last line of quilting. Bind (see page 20).

Single Blocks in Appliqué

ant to try a design? Why not stitch a single block? Here are a handful of appliquéd creations. Pinwheel, bright and cheery. Log Cabin, always a favorite. Card Tricks, eye popping. Shoo-Fly, see how different quilting and appliqué placement can change the look of the work. Ohio Star, a touch of lace and beads make it special. And Flying Iris, an appliquéd and quilted version of the well-known Flying Geese pattern. These will get you started. Soon you will be creating quilted blocks by the dozens.

Materials

Background muslin, cut a piece 1" larger all around than the block size, for example, 9" x 9" for the Pinwheel block.

Batting and backing, cut 1" larger all around than the top.

Full-size working pattern for each block.

Exception: make a 5 block, full-size pattern for the Flying Iris.

Embroidery floss for the details

Fabrics, these are great projects to use up those bits and pieces.

Additional unique items as noted in Special Instructions per Block.

Directions (for all)

No dot template is needed for single blocks. Draw a five block working pattern for the Flying Iris and single block working pattern for all the others.

Spray starch the background fabric. Center the fabric over the working pattern. Using a removable marker and the lightbox, mark the reference dots and appliqué design. Mark the reference dots with thread.

Appliqué the design (see page 14). Embroider the details. Refer to Special Instructions per Block on the next page. Remove all marks but leave the thread dots. Press well from the back.

Return the block to the working pattern and align the thread dots, using some pins to secure the fabric to the pattern. Using a removable marker, trace the quilting lines.

Baste the three layers (top, batting, and backing) together for quilting (see page 19). Quilt the marked design as well as around the appliquéd pieces (see page 20). Remove all marks, thread dots, and basting threads. Trim the outer edges 1/2" from the last line of quilting. Bind (see page 20).

Special Instructions per Block

Pinwheel

Embroider the stems with a green stem stitch. Add four yellow and one black French knot to the flower centers.

Log Cabin

Embroider the stems with green stem stitch. Dot the berries with white French knots. To the cranberries add a single stitch in black at the flower end and a short white crescent in stem stitch on the berries.

Card Tricks

Use black single straight stitches for the stamens. End each stamen with a white French knot. Stem stitch the stems in green.

Shoo-Fly

Both versions. Embroider the leaf stems in green stem stitch. Run a line of quilting around the top edge of the sunflower center.

Ohio Star

Embroider the antennae in black using a single strand of floss in stem stitch. Satin stitch the butterfly bodies in black. Add three French knots to the top of each flower head. After quilting, stitch on a bead for each butterfly head and a small piece of lace for the outer wing.

Flying Iris

Embroider the stem with two parallel rows of stem stitch in green. Use yellow single straight stitches for the pollen lines in the flower centers. Add a single black French knot to each flower center.

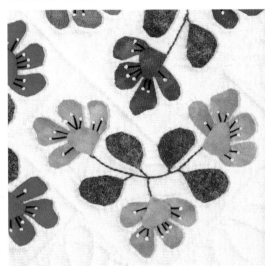

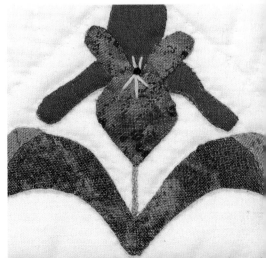

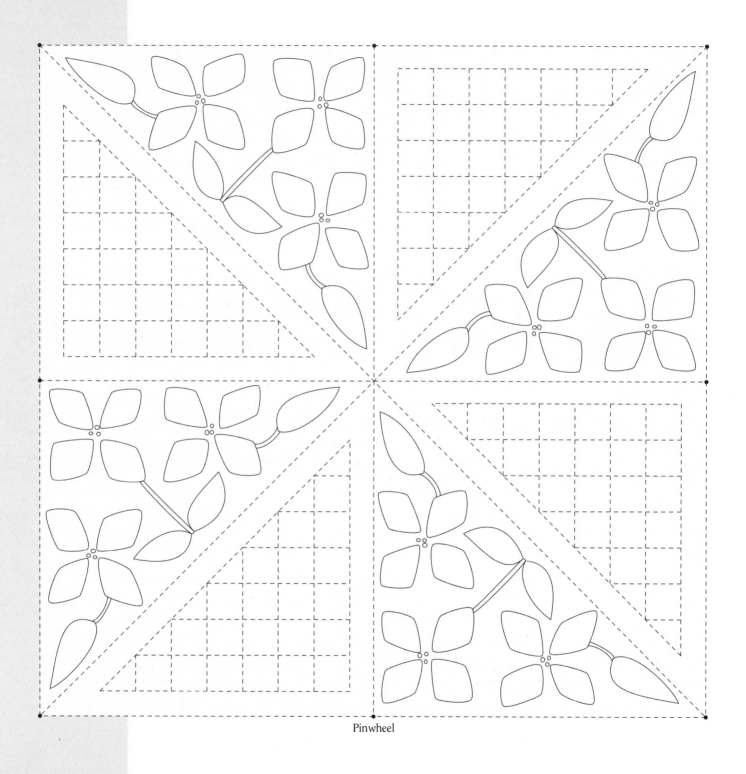

Pinwheel

Pinwheel 8" x 8"

Log Cabin–enlarge 125% to 8³⁄₄" x 8³⁄₄"

Log Cabin 9³/₄" x 9³/₄"

Card Tricks–enlarge 125% to 9" x 9"

Card Tricks 10" x 10"

Shoo-Fly, two versions–enlarge 135% to 9" x 9"

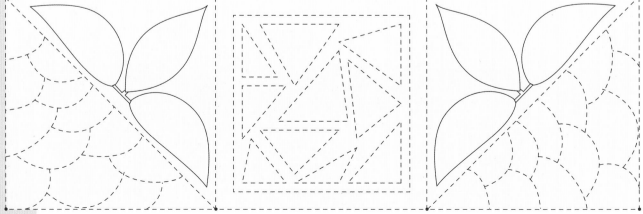

Shoo-Fly, two versions 10" x 10"

Ohio Star—enlarge 125% to 9" x 9"

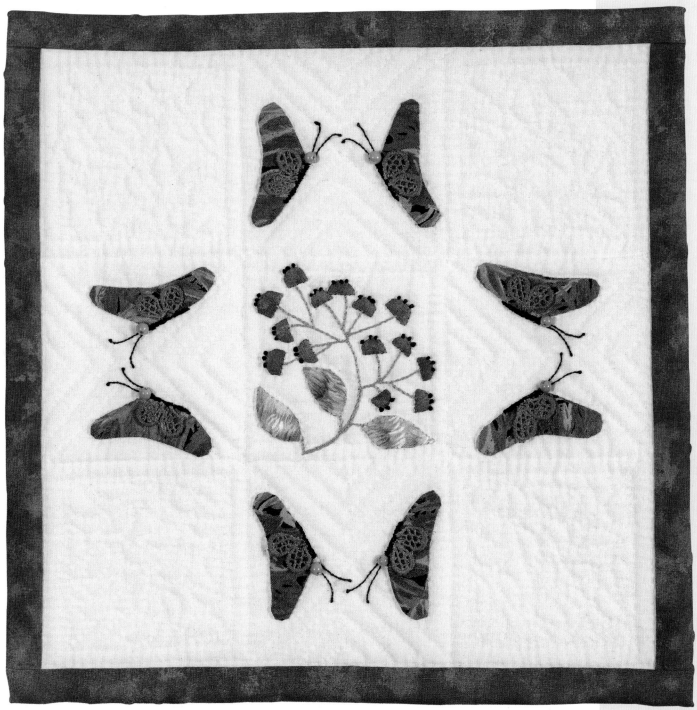

Ohio Star 10" x 10"

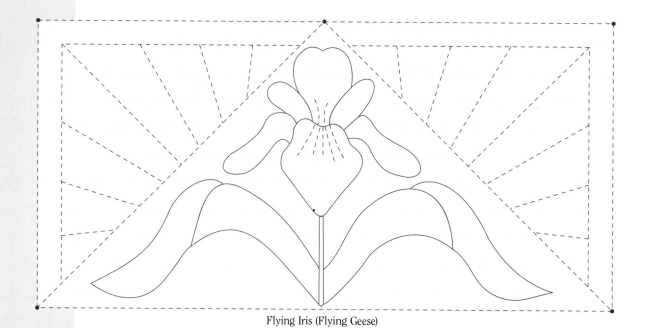

Flying Iris (Flying Geese)

Flying Iris (Flying Geese) 7″ x 16″

About the Author

Carol Armstrong taught herself to quilt in 1980, developing her unique and highly artistic style. She uses her favorite technique, "Lightbox Appliqué." Conventionalized botanical celebrations of flora and birds are her strongest output, though any subject that catches her artistic eye may end up a minutely detailed grace on fabric.

In 1986, Carol moved to Michigan's Upper Peninsula, where she lives with her cabinetmaker husband, J.M. Friedrich, in the country near Shingleton. Carol says the wonderfully snowy winters give her time to quilt while her husband "Red" makes fine craft items in his workshop. When her fingers and eyes need a diversion, there is always water to pump and bring in the house, wood to load into the woodbox, bird feeders to fill, or the large organic vegetable garden to tend.

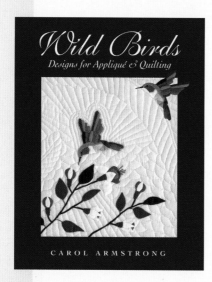

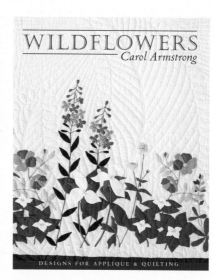

Carol presents charming images inspired by her personal observations of nature. Appliqué these designs of your favorite feathered friends onto quilts, clothing, and home decor items.

Mix and match 24 wildflower patterns. Instructions for 10 projects and Carol's innovative free-form quilting designs.

Index

Other Fine Books from C&T Publishing

250 Continuous-Line Quilting Designs for Hand, Machine & Long-Arm Quilters, Laura Lee Fritz

Along the Garden Path: More Quilters and Their Gardens, Jean and Valori Wells

An Amish Adventure: 2nd Edition, Roberta Horton

Anatomy of a Doll: The Fabric Sculptor's Handbook, Susanna Oroyan

Appliqué 12 Easy Ways! Charming Quilts, Giftable Projects & Timeless Techniques, Elly Sienkiewicz

The Art of Machine Piecing: Quality Workmanship Through a Colorful Journey, Sally Collins

The Art of Silk Ribbon Embroidery, Judith Baker Montano

The Art of Classic Quiltmaking, Harriet Hargrave and Sharyn Craig

The Artful Ribbon, Candace Kling

Baltimore Beauties and Beyond (Volume I), Elly Sienkiewicz

The Best of Baltimore Beauties, Elly Sienkiewicz

Block Magic: Over 50 Fun & Easy Blocks from Squares and Rectangles, Nancy Johnson-Srebro

Civil War Women: Their Quilts, Their Roles, and Activities for Re-Enactors, Barbara Brackman

Color From the Heart: Seven Great Ways to Make Quilts with Colors You Love, Gai Perry

Color Play: Easy Steps to Imaginative Color in Quilts, Joen Wolfrom

Cotton Candy Quilts: Using Feedsacks, Vintage and Reproduction Fabrics, Mary Mashuta

Crazy Quilt Handbook, 2nd Edition, Judith Montano

Crazy with Cotton, Diana Leone

Curves in Motion: Quilt Designs & Techniques, Judy B. Dales

Cut-Loose Quilts: Stack, Slice, Switch & Sew, Jan Mullen

Designing the Doll: From Concept to Construction, Susanna Oroyan

Diane Phalen Quilts: 10 Projects to Celebrate the Seasons, Diane Phalen

Do-It-Yourself Framed Quilts: Fast, Fun & Easy Projects, Gai Perry

Easy Pieces: Creative Color Play with Two Simple Blocks, Margaret Miller

Elegant Stitches: An Illustrated Stitch Guide & Source Book of Inspiration, Judith Baker Montano

Everything Flowers: Quilts from the Garden, Jean and Valori Wells

Exploring Machine Trapunto: New Dimensions, Hari Walner

Fabric Shopping with Alex Anderson, Seven Projects to Help You: Make Successful Choices, Build Your Confidence, Add to Your Fabric Stash, Alex Anderson

Fancy Appliqué: 12 Lessons to Enhance Your Skills, Elly Sienkiewicz

Fantastic Fabric Folding: Innovative Quilting Projects, Rebecca Wat

Fantastic Figures: Ideas & Techniques Using the New Clays, Susanna Oroyan

Finishing the Figure: Doll Costuming • Embellishments • Accessories, Susanna Oroyan

Floral Stitches: An Illustrated Guide, Judith Baker Montano

Flower Pounding: Quilt Projects for All Ages, Amy Sandrin & Ann Frischkorn

Freddy's House: Brilliant Color in Quilts, Freddy Moran

Free Stuff for Crafty Kids on the Internet, Judy Heim and Gloria Hansen

Free Stuff for Doll Lovers on the Internet, Judy Heim and Gloria Hansen

Free Stuff for Gardeners on the Internet, Judy Heim and Gloria Hansen

Free Stuff for Home Décor on the Internet, Judy Heim and Gloria Hansen

Free Stuff for Home Repair on the Internet, Judy Heim and Gloria Hansen

Free Stuff for Pet Lovers on the Internet, Gloria Hansen

Free Stuff for Quilters on the Internet, 3rd Ed., Judy Heim and Gloria Hansen

Free Stuff for Scrapbooking on the Internet, Judy Heim and Gloria Hansen

Free Stuff for Sewing Fanatics on the Internet, Judy Heim and Gloria Hansen

Free Stuff for Stitchers on the Internet, Judy Heim and Gloria Hansen

Free Stuff for Traveling Quilters on the Internet, Gloria Hansen

Free-Style Quilts: A "No Rules" Approach, Susan Carlson

Ghost Layers & Color Washes: Three Steps to Spectacular Quilts, Katie Pasquini Masopust

Great Lakes, Great Quilts: 12 Projects Celebrating Quilting Traditions, Marsha MacDowell

Hand Appliqué with Alex Anderson: Seven Projects for Hand Appliqué, Alex Anderson

Hand Quilting with Alex Anderson: Six Projects for Hand Quilters, Alex Anderson

Heirloom Machine Quilting, Third Edition, Harriet Hargrave

Impressionist Palette, Gai Perry

Impressionist Quilts, Gai Perry

In the Nursery: Creative Quilts and Designer Touches, Jennifer Sampou & Carolyn Schmitz

Kaleidoscopes: Wonders of Wonder, Cozy Baker

Kaleidoscopes & Quilts, Paula Nadelstern

Laurel Burch Quilts: Kindred Creatures, Laurel Burch

Lone Star Quilts and Beyond: Projects and Inspiration, Jan Krentz

Machine Embroidery and More: Ten Step-by-Step Projects Using Border Fabrics & Beads, Kristen Dibbs

Magical Four-Patch and Nine-Patch Quilts, Yvonne Porcella

Make Any Block Any Size, Joen Wolfrom

Mastering Machine Appliqué, Harriet Hargrave

Mastering Quilt Marking: Marking Tools & Techniques, Choosing Stencils, Matching Borders & Corners, Pepper Cory

The New Sampler Quilt, Diana Leone

On the Surface: Thread Embellishment & Fabric Manipulation, Wendy Hill

Patchwork Persuasion: Fascinating Quilts from Traditional Designs, Joen Wolfrom

The Photo Transfer Handbook: Snap It, Print It, Stitch It!, Jean Ray Laury

Pieced Flowers, Ruth B. McDowell

Piecing: Expanding the Basics, Ruth B. McDowell

Plaids & Stripes: The Use of Directional Fabrics in Quilts, Roberta Horton

Quilt It for Kids: 11 Projects, Sports, Fantasy & Animal Themes, Quilts for Children of All Ages, Pam Bono

Quilted Memories: Celebrations of Life, Mary Lou Weidman

The Quilted Garden: Design & Make Nature-Inspired Quilts, Jane A. Sassaman

Quilting Back to Front: Fun & Easy No-Mark Techniques, Larraine Scouler

For more information write for a free catalog:

C&T Publishing, Inc.
P. O. Box 1456
Lafayette, CA 94549
(800) 284-1114
e-mail: ctinfo@ctpub.com
website: www.ctpub.com

For quilting supplies:

Cotton Patch Mail Order
3405 Hall Lane, Dept. CTB
Lafayette, CA 94549
(800) 835-4418
(925) 283-7883
e-mail: quiltusa@yahoo.com
website: www.quiltusa.com

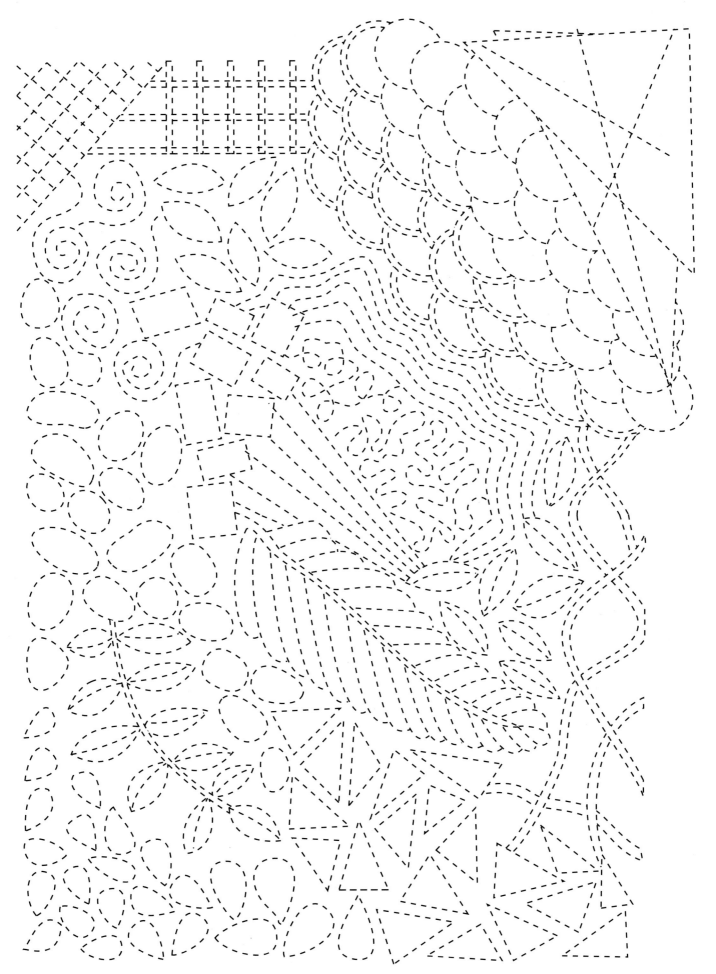

95